A PARENT'S GUIDE TO
DRUGS

JUDY MACKIE

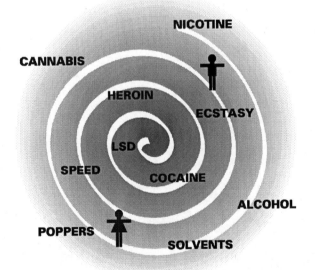

NICOTINE

CANNABIS

HEROIN

ECSTASY

LSD

SPEED   COCAINE

ALCOHOL

POPPERS

SOLVENTS

Need2Know

REAL INFORMATION AND PRACTICAL ADVICE

362.29

First published by Need2Know 1997
Need2Know, Remus House, Woodston,
Peterborough PE2 9JX

Contents

Introduction

'Schoolboy in drugs probe found hanged'
'Teenage drug shock'
'Kids aged 9 score heroin'
'Junkie kids get high'

Do these headlines look familiar? They should do - they're typical of the sorts of stories found every day in both the tabloid and broadsheet press. Add to that the graphically sordid experiences of young addicts in cult films such as *Trainspotting*; the regular drug storylines of the popular TV soaps, and the ongoing political campaigns to crack down on pushers - and the picture painted is of a society pockmarked with needle holes and full of drug-induced crime and despair.

Not surprisingly, parents are frightened by such a perception, perpetuated by all forms of media on a daily basis.

- How can they protect their children against the horrors of heroin and other hard drugs?
- How will they know if their child has fallen prey?
- What can they do to stop them sliding down the slippery slope towards addiction, bad health, and social problems?

Well, the first step is to get a grip on reality, or 'get real', as your child would probably say. The myths surrounding drugs and drug use can be as bizarre as any chemically-induced hallucination - and probably far more damaging to the way we live our lives and communicate with others.

Mistrust and misunderstandings based on these myths build barriers between generations and do nothing towards addressing the real problems - both health-related and social - caused by drugs.

Yes, we live in a drug-taking society. Very few youngsters will not be exposed to drugs in some form or another during their formative years. New drugs have appeared on the scene and children are experimenting at an earlier age. But all these facts should be kept in perspective.

One of the biggest myths around is that use of hard drugs, such as heroin, crack and cocaine is rife among young people throughout the UK. In fact, heroin users account for only around 1% of the total number of drug users in this country, and use of cocaine and crack account for no more than 2%.

According to surveys of different regions, by far the most popular drug among UK youngsters is cannabis (80-90%), which is not physically addictive and cannot be overdosed on. The second most popular drug is ecstasy (10-15%), followed by LSD and speed (amphetamine).

Each of these drugs carries its own particular risks, as we shall discover in later chapters. But they are far from close to transforming an entire generation of young people into hopeless addicts with no future.

This book aims to help you as a parent to separate the myths from the realities and form a clearer perception of the drug culture and why it is so attractive to youngsters.

Together, we'll look at different drugs and their effects, described first-hand by young users themselves; we'll discover what other parents and young people think about drugs; we'll consider the legal implications of drug use, and we'll learn what to do about coping with drug emergencies and seeking professional support.

This knowledge is very important, because you have a key role to play in educating your children about drugs. You have the greatest understanding of and influence over your child's life. You know their likes, dislikes, needs, idiosyncrasies, fears and triumphs. National and local anti-drugs campaigns are undoubtedly useful, but when it comes to getting through to young people on an individual basis, you know better than any teacher, counsellor or health promoter what will and won't wash with your child.

Communication is the key to helping young people make the decisions that are right for them. And that doesn't mean giving long lectures about drugs, or instigating the Spanish Inquisition every time they come home from a night out! Listening to your child, making time to chat about what's happening in his or her life on a regular basis, and generally building a good relationship with them, will provide them with a strong and trustworthy base to return to when they want support or someone to talk things through with.

Most parents will argue that talking about talking to teenagers is far easier than putting it into practice, with such distractions as TV, computer games, and other leisure activities to compete with. But good communication can be learned. If you are having difficulty talking to your child, this book will help you get started. Our practical guide will take you through the basic steps, which you can use and develop to suit your own individual circumstances. And of course, these skills don't apply only to discussions on drugs. They will help you build better relationships within your family, based on trust and mutual respect.

One of the first steps to good communication is honesty. And when it comes to talking about drugs, that's where parents can fall down quite heavily. If you smoke and or drink alcohol, you are liable to be attacked as a hypocrite if you attempt to advise your child on the perils of taking drugs. Unlike older generations, young people see cigarettes and drink as drugs like any other - so be prepared to be challenged on your own drug use!

Having climbed down from our pedestals, we're now in a better position to tackle the subject of drugs and their myriad effects on those who use them. Forget the media scare-stories and stereotypes. It's time to open your mind and fasten your seatbelt - here's the deal for real.

1 SETTING THE SCENE

- New trends
- Young people
- Under-16s
- Why the increase in drug-taking?
- Summing up...

One of the main reasons we as a society tend to panic about drugs is our collective fear of the unknown. The best horror screenwriters know that the monster which is never revealed is far scarier than the one which even the most sizzling Spielberg special effects can produce. And because many people still have little or no knowledge of illicit drugs and their effects, these have grown hideous in the public's imagination.

Up to very recently, and compared to the information which has long been available on the use and effects of alcohol and tobacco, there has been a dearth of UK-wide statistical data gathered on drugs. As a result, a shroud of mystery still surrounds the facts about drug-taking trends. Thankfully, since the late 1980s, several large-scale regional surveys have been carried out and, together with the most recent British Crime Survey (1994), which carries a section on illicit drug use in England and Wales, and a new survey of young people throughout the UK, these can give us a broad picture of the latest trends.

New Trends

The most significant finding is that drug-taking has escalated dramatically within only a few years.

- The British Crime Survey (BCS) reveals that half of all men aged 16-29 admit to have taken drugs at some time in their lives - a 50% increase on the 1992 BCS figures

- Nearly three in 10 people in England and Wales have taken drugs (two-thirds more than in 1992)

- Although only one in 10 said they had taken them within the last year, this was again a two-thirds increase on 1992

- So, around nine million people aged between 16 and 59 will have taken a drug at some time in their life, and about two million will have taken a drug in the past month

- By far the most widely-used drug is cannabis, with 6.3 million people having used it at some time in their life, and nearly 1.5 million having used it in the last month

- After cannabis, the three most popular drugs within the 16-59 age group are amphetamine (nearly 2.5 million in their lifetime; 303,000 in the last month); LSD (1.3 million; 152,00) and ecstasy (728,000; 121,000)

- Less than one per cent of the population use heroin

Young People

- Those in the 16-19 age bracket were much more likely to have taken drugs within the last month than older age ranges

- After cannabis, those who reported recent drug use chose amphetamine (6%), LSD (3%) and poppers (3%)

- A significant new trend, which has not appeared in any previous survey and is not reflected in any of the other BCS age brackets, is that young women aged 16-19 are almost equally as likely as men to have used drugs at some time in their lives (46% women; 48% men)

- More teenage women than men now use solvents

- Both sexes use equal amounts of poppers (16%), LSD (12%), ecstasy (8%) and cocaine (3%)

- Heroin use among the younger age range did not exceed 1%, either within the last month or within a lifetime

Under-16s

But what about the drug-taking habits of youngsters under 16? While research has shown that those in the 16-29 age range are far more likely to take drugs than under-16s, the drug use among younger members of the population is also steadily increasing.

- In 1989, 11.1% of youngsters had tried an illicit drug by age 16; in 1991 the figure had doubled to 22.3%; by 1993 it was 33.4% and the latest figures show this has now reached an average of 43% across England, Scotland and Wales

- A comprehensive study of 7722 schoolchildren aged 15-16 throughout the UK* revealed that school-age drug use is most prevalent in Scotland (55%), followed by England (41%), Wales (33%) and Northern Ireland (26%)

- Predictably, the most popular drug is cannabis (Scotland - 53%, England - 40%, Wales -32%, Northern Ireland - 23%), but the survey also highlighted a relatively high level of use of solvents (Northern Ireland- 26%, Scotland 22%, England 20%, Wales 18%)

- Studies carried out between 1988 and 1993** have also shown a considerable increase in the use of cannabis (2%-16%), LSD, amphetamine and magic mushrooms (from below 1% to 5%-7%) among 14-15-year-olds, with around 3% using ecstasy in 1993

All these figures are general and although they are the latest available, some may already be out of date. It also shouldn't be forgotten that drug-taking trends, like the slang names of drugs themselves, do vary considerably from region to region within the UK. For example, the practice of injecting temazapan ('jellies') in Scotland is virtually unknown in England, and crack/cocaine is at the moment a far greater problem in some parts of England than it is elsewhere in the UK.

If you would like a clearer picture of trends in your own area, ask your local health authority or drugs agency for some statistics (see Help List, Pages 101-103 for further details).

Why the increase in drug-taking?

The short answer to this is 'because the drugs are there'. Never before have so many different types of drugs been so easily available in the UK. The illegal drugs industry is a multi-billion, world-wide concern, which is showing little signs of abating. It seems that nearly every other day we hear of huge hauls of heroin, cocaine/crack and cannabis being intercepted by the authorities - yet they will be the first to admit that this is only the tip of the iceberg.

Being so readily available, drugs are reasonably cheap (see Chapter Three). Young people who want to buy them have both the money and the opportunity to do so. It stands to reason that the more easily available drugs are, the greater the likelihood that increasing numbers of youngsters will at least experiment with them. We'll come back to the ways in which we can all help to tackle this, in Chapter Five.

But to get back to the issue of increasing drug use, it can also to a great extent be attributed to the rise of the youth dance/rave culture during the late 1980s and throughout the 1990s. Just as drugs played a major 'mind-expanding' role in the music revolutions of the 1960s and 1970s, they are doing so in the house, jungle and grunge music so popular today. Drugs such as LSD, ecstasy and amphetamine have for many young people become an inextricable part of partying, and this has been reinforced by certain sections of the mass youth market, through music, clothes, books and films.

Summing up...

- Looking at why drug use has increased so much in recent years is a little like puzzling over the chicken and egg scenario - is the increase due to the wide availability of drugs and the lure of new drugs (or new variations of existing drugs), or has the drugs industry, just like any other, expanded due to increasing consumer demand? Which came first? Or have both developed in tandem?

- Leaving the experts to argue this one out - and the law enforcement agencies to continue to crack down on the suppliers - the main concern for the rest of us is, in the face of such widespread drug use, what can we do? The good news is there is much we can do, and the first important step is to ensure we have our facts straight about drugs. Now that we have a general idea of the UK drugs scene today, it's time to tackle some of the biggest obstacles to achieving a better understanding of drugs - the myths.

Footnotes

- R Miller P and Plant M: *Drinking, Smoking and Illicit Drug Use Among 15 and 16 Year Olds in the United Kingdom.*

- R Balding J: *Young People in 1993*

2 DRUGS - THE MYTHS

- I know nothing
- Dangerous assumptions
- Don't tell me about young people
- Us and them
- Paying the price
- It's good to talk
- Searching questions
- Summing up...

Before we take a look at individual drugs and their effects, let's get a few things straight. Have your mallets at the ready, because here is where some of the most commonly-believed myths about drugs get a good bashing...

I Know Nothing

I don't know anything about drugs...

Oh yes you do! You may never have touched an illegal drug, but the chances are you have smoked or drunk alcohol at some stage, and perhaps still do. A lot can be learned from your own use of alcohol or tobacco - or prescribed drugs such as sleeping tablets or anti-depressants, for that matter. If you think about it carefully, you may find that this use falls into some sort of pattern, becoming more pronounced during certain times of your life. Your reasons for choosing to use legal drugs may be similar to those which prompt young people to use illegal drugs. So the gap between you isn't as wide as you think!

- Be honest about your own 'drug career'. Remember your own teenage years - did you pay any attention to your parents' attitudes to going out, drinking, etc? If so, how did they get through to you? If not, were they too heavy-handed? Bear all this in mind when trying to communicate with your child about drugs.

Dangerous Assumptions

All drugs are dangerous...

Thankfully, this is not the case, otherwise hospitals could not cope with the number of people needing urgent attention. Although there are certain risks attached to every drug - legal or illegal - most people who use drugs will come to little or no physical harm. More about risks in Chapter 3.

Illegal drugs are more dangerous than cigarettes and alcohol...

Alcohol and tobacco account for more deaths than illegal drugs: around 30,000 deaths a year can be attributed to alcohol, while smoking kills around 111,000 people annually.

One try of hard drugs, such as heroin or cocaine, is enough to get you hooked...

Although it is easier to become dependent on heroin and

cocaine than on other drugs, it takes time to develop a dependency. As with trying alcohol or smoking for the first time, trying drugs doesn't mean instant addiction. Even when dependent - either psychologically, physically or both - most drug users do eventually give up or control their use. More about dependency in Chapter 3.

Cannabis is addictive...

You can't become physically dependent on cannabis, although some people become dependent on it psychologically, ie to help them cope with everyday life. For more information about this drug and its effects, see Chapter 3.

Cannabis is harmless...

This is a widely-believed myth. Some people do become psychologically dependent on cannabis, and, if smoked, it can also damage the lungs. Driving under the influence of cannabis is as dangerous as drink-driving, and the legal implications of getting caught in possession of the drug could ruin a young person's career.

Ecstasy kills...

Tragically, some young people have died from taking just one tablet of ecstasy. To date, there have been around 50 deaths of this kind in the UK. The majority of these have been as a result of dehydration through a combination of increased body temperature due both to the drug itself and to prolonged dancing in a hot atmosphere. This is why advice has been given about drinking plenty of water.

However, following a recent death which occurred as a result of drinking too much water, there has been a lot of confusion over this advice. In this case, the drug caused an increase in Anti-Diuretic Hormone (ADH), which makes the body retain water, which led to the brain swelling due to excess water in the body.

The message now given to young people who use ecstasy is to drink water only if they are dancing (and therefore losing water through sweat. To put the dangers of ecstasy in perspective, hundreds of thousands of the tablets are taken every week in the UK, with no dangerous effects. But it is important to know that there is growing evidence to suggest that ecstasy has long-term psychological effects. For more about ecstasy and its effects, see Chapter 3.

Soft drugs inevitably lead to hard drugs...

Although most heroin users will have tried cannabis at some stage, it is not the case that most cannabis users will go on to experiment with heroin.

- Try not to see drug issues in black and white. Being too judgmental from the start won't encourage two-way discussion with your child.

Don't Tell Me About Young People...

Young people take drugs because they are bored...
It's not as clear-cut as that. There are plenty of young

people who have full and active lives, who also experiment with drugs.

They're put under pressure to try drugs by their friends...
The urge to be the same as their friends may encourage some young people to try drugs, but they still usually do it through choice, rather than pressure. Teenagers who choose not to take drugs or alcohol are more often respected, rather than ridiculed, by their peers.

- Give your child credit for thinking for him/herself. Blaming their friends will only alienate them from you. Encourage them to bring friends home, so that you get to know them as people - not rivals for your child's affection. That way, you'll be able to judge whether or not they really are a 'bad influence'. What's more important is that knowing about your child's friends gives you something in common and helps strengthen your relationship.

Us And Them

Drug-taking happens only in deprived areas...
Not true. There is clear evidence that drugs are used throughout society, by people of all backgrounds and classes.

If youngsters take drugs, their parents must be to blame...
As we've seen, young people of all ages, classes and

backgrounds take drugs for all sorts of reasons - positive and negative. Most of them choose to do so of their own free will, and their upbringing has nothing to do with it.

'Normal' youngsters don't take drugs...

If you mean that only young people with serious problems take drugs, that's not true. Drug use need not necessarily signify an inability to cope - it is also regarded as recreational by many young people: something that's fun and makes them feel good.

- Drugs are a great equaliser in society - there's no room for snobbish complacency!

Paying The Price

Most drug users turn to crime to finance their habit...

Drug users who turn to crime tend to be dependent on heroin, crack or cocaine - drugs which are not popular among young people. Most young drug users are not dependent and can afford to buy drugs without having to steal to pay for them.

But surely drugs are very expensive..?

Not those commonly used by young people. As little as £5 will buy a bottle of 'poppers' or a tab of LSD; £10 will buy a 'wrap' of amphetamine or enough cannabis for four joints; a tablet of ecstasy may cost £12-£25; magic mushrooms grow wild in September/October, and solvents are cheap and freely available in shops.

- It pays to stay streetwise about the realities of drug-taking. Knowing the facts and figures will give you better credibility with your child.

It's Good To Talk

We need to be stricter with our kids...
Being too strict can have the opposite effect.

Scare tactics put youngsters off trying drugs...
Research has shown that scare tactics don't work. When young people discover drugs are not the instantaneous killers they are made out to be, they don't trust anything we say and may then start to believe that drugs are harmless. They, like all of us, need to be told the truth about drugs so that they can make informed decisions.

That's right - once they know the facts, they won't experiment with drugs...
If it were only that simple! While knowing the facts about drugs may make them more careful, it won't necessarily stop them using drugs. As adults we know the risks associated with smoking and drinking, but that doesn't necessarily stop us using tobacco and alcohol. But knowledge is empowering, and young people who are well-informed about drugs are less likely to come to serious harm.

Discussing drugs with children might encourage them to try them...

This is not true. If you don't talk to your child about drugs, you can be sure that they will find out about them anyway. Isn't it better for them to hear the truth from you than half-truths from a less accurate source?

But they're too young...

It's never too early to start talking to children about drugs, as long as you do it in a way that's appropriate for their age. Don't rely on teachers to take sole responsibility for your child's drug education. Parents, more than any other adult, have an enormous influence over their children.

- If certain subjects have always been taboo in your family, you'll find it far harder to discuss them when you decide it's finally time to bring them into the open. But don't worry if you fall into this category - all is not lost. See Chapter 6 for some basic communication tips.

Searching Questions

You can easily tell if your child is using drugs...

Unless you see them high on drugs, it's almost impossible to tell. Think about it: many of the signs associated with drug-taking - such as mood swings, lack of appetite, tiredness and suspicious behaviour - can also be attributed to normal teenage life! In Chapter Eight, we'll cover these signs in greater depth, but these are by no means clear-cut evidence that drugs have been used.

If I knew what these drugs looked like, I might be able to tell if my child was using them...

It's very unlikely that your child would leave drugs lying around for you to find! Another problem is that the same drugs come in different sizes, shapes and colours. Our guide to drugs in common use in Chapter 3 will help you identify the most popular forms, but don't count on ever finding any - most young people use drugs outside the home. It's also important to remember that snooping around their bedroom will not help your relationship...

- Rather than becoming obsessed with searching for signs of drug use, concentrate on building a trusting relationship with your child. That way, if there is any reason to suspect they're using drugs, you'll be in a far stronger position to talk to them about it and, if necessary, give them advice and guidance.

Summing up...

Well, did you recognise any of your own thoughts, fears and beliefs among these myths? It wouldn't be surprising, considering we are all exposed on a daily basis to misconceptions about drugs and what they do.

But we won't be misled in future, will we? Now we've ditched our preconceptions and prejudices, we can take the facts on board and look at drugs in a more rational, objective manner.

You might find what you're about to read in the next few chapters rather unsettling - perhaps even shocking - as we explore the realities of drugs and drug users. But far better to know and face up to what's actually happening than live in a fictitious world of terrifying tabloid headlines!

3 WHAT ARE WE DEALING WITH?

- A comprehensive guide to drugs and their effects
- Stimulants
- Depressants
- Hallucinogens
- Solvents
- Alcohol
- Nicotine
- Summing up...

If all drugs were to be made legal and sold in the high street, their sheer variety of shapes, colours and associated paraphernalia would make a weird and fascinating shop window display, guaranteed to halt passers-by in their tracks.

Let's take a peek into the 'shop window' of drugs easily obtainable in the UK today. The two which cause most damage within our society appear at the end of the list. Look at how their effects and risks compare with those of the others and you'll perhaps understand why adults can appear hypocritical when warning young people about the dangers of taking drugs.

Type	Effect
Stimulants	Drugs which speed everything up, including thoughts, speech and physical movement.
Depressants	Drugs which slow everything down.
Hallucinogens	Alter a person's perception of reality, causing hallucinations and confusion.

Stimulants

Ecstasy

- Other names: E, white doves, disco burgers

- Ecstasy (methylenedioxymeth-amphetamine, or MDMA) became popular in the UK during the late 1980s, with the advent of house music and the rave culture. Many young people now see the drug as an inextricable part of the dance scene and it has been cleverly marketed as such. Song lyrics glorify E as an escape-valve to love and freedom, and the pulsating atmosphere of dance clubs and raves, where youngsters dance non-stop with their friends in a kaleidoscopic haze of shifting colours and light, is condusive to the euphoric and energy-enhancing effects of the drug.

  In the UK, around 500,000 people - and by no means all of them teenagers - regularly use ecstasy for recreational purposes. It is normally sold as a white, brown, pink or yellow tablet, or coloured capsule, fetching between £12 and £25 each.

- The up side: 'When I take eccie it makes me think the music

I'm listening to is the best I've ever heard in my life. If I've been arguing with someone, the anger suddenly goes away. It makes me so happy.' (14-year-old boy)

- Enjoyable effects: 'rushes' of exhilaration and euphoria; sensations are enhanced; inhibitions are lowered; users may experience a warm feeling of universal love and friendship.

- Duration: 3-4 hours.

- The down side:

  Users may overheat without realising (see Chapter 2).

  Very little is known about the long-term effects of ecstasy. It is not believed to cause physical dependence, but regular users do develop a tolerance and may become anxious, confused and subject to insomnia.

- May cause liver damage.

- As it acts as a stimulant on the metabolism, people with heart conditions, high blood pressure, epilepsy or any kind of mental illness should avoid using it.

Amphetamine

- Other names: speed, uppers, sulph, whizz

- Amphetamine is the second most commonly used drug in the UK (next to cannabis), and became notorious as a 'stay-awake' party drug used by Mods during the early 60s. There are many types of amphetamine, but the most commonly used today is amphetamine sulphate.

- Amphetamine usually comes in the form of a white powder (but can be obtained in other coloured powder or tablet form), which can be snorted (sniffed), rubbed on the gums, dissolved in a drink, or mixed with water and injected. Buyers are often short-changed by dealers, who may 'cut' the drug with other substances such as sugar or bicarbonate of soda. A 'wrap'(small paper packet) of speed will cost around £10-£15 per gram.

- The up side: 'Speed makes my heart beat really quickly. It makes me go like a whippet. I can stay awake all night and all the next day no problem.' (13-year-old boy).

- Enjoyable effects: sensations of alertness, confidence and well-being; raises levels of energy and stamina; lessens desire to eat and sleep.

- Duration: 3-4 hours.

- The down side:

  Speed may cause psychological dependence and users may quickly develop a tolerance, resorting to increasingly larger doses.

  Long-term use may result in disturbed sleep, uncomfortable itching, acute anxiety or paranoia, loss of appetite and aggressive behaviour.

  High blood pressure and calcium deficiency are also common among amphetamine users, and those who rub it into their gums may lose their teeth.

  Injecting the drug carries a number of risks - it may have been cut with other substances which could damage the veins and internal organs; sharing dirty needles may spread HIV and hepatitis, and injecting into an artery rather than a vein could cause gangrene.

  For heavy users, the comedown can be unpleasant (although not physically dangerous) and may cause symptoms such as hunger, lethargy and depression.

Cocaine

- Other names: coke, snow, charlie.

- Cocaine, which is extracted from the leaf of the South American coca plant, has been used recreationally for centuries, but was recognised as an addictive drug and banned from all but medical use in the US during the early 1900s. It became popular once again in the mid-1960s and is today widely available on the UK streets, although its high price makes it less popular with young people.

  Cocaine most commonly comes in the form of cocaine hydrochloride - a white, crystalline powder, which, like speed, is often cut with other substances. The drug is usually snorted, but is sometimes injected. A gram of 'coke' will cost anything from £50 to £100.

- The up side: 'I've only ever done two lines, and the only word I can use to describe coke is it makes you feel jellied...out of it.' (14-year-old boy).

- Enjoyable effects: causes powerful sensations of alertness and confidence.

- Duration: Up to 30 minutes.

- The down side:

  Cocaine may cause psychological, and possibly physical, dependence.

  Blood pressure can be increased to the extent of causing a stroke.

  Too much sniffing can damage the lining of the nose.

  Excessive doses can produce anxiety, sweating, dizziness, dry mouth, trembling hands and ringing ears.

  Long-term use can irreversibly damage nerves and small blood vessels in the brain.

  Heavy doses can cause frightening hallucinations and delusions.

  'Coming down' can be very unpleasant. Withdrawal may

result in depression.

Crack

- Other names: rock, pebbles.

- Crack, a very powerful form of cocaine which has been chemically separated from hydrochloride, first became available on US streets in the mid-1980s. It is gradually becoming more popular in Britain, but is still relatively rare.

  Crack comes in crystals, or 'rocks', which are smoked in a pipe, or heated on tin foil and inhaled. A small crystal costs around £20.

- The up side: 'I smoked it and got this instant rush, a fantastic high which made the hairs rise on the back of my neck. It was like taking speed, but far more powerful.' (29-year-old male).

- Enjoyable effects: these have been described as being like 'a thousand simultaneous orgasms'.

- Duration: Around 10 minutes.

- The down side:

  Like cocaine, crack may cause psychological, and possibly physical, dependence, and users run the same risks.

  The effects wear off rapidly, leaving users irritable, depressed and wanting to repeat the experience.

  Smoking crack is damaging to the lungs and may cause severe chest pains, bronchitis and asthma.

  Crack has been described by police as one of the worst drugs around, due to its tendency to induce violent behaviour in users desperate for money to buy more.

Amyl and Butyl Nitrate

- Other names: poppers, rush, locker room.

- Amyl and Butyl Nitrate are vapours which, when inhaled, dilate the blood vessels and give an instant 'rush'. Available from clubs, bars and sex shops, they are used by people of all ages, often to enhance sexual pleasure.

  Poppers come in small flip-top plastic or metallic bottles, carrying names such as 'Liquid Gold' or 'New Hit', and costing between £3 and £6 a bottle.

- The up side: 'When you take poppers your head throbs and you think it's going to explode. Then it goes numb for a couple of minutes. You're supposed to keep it in your bedroom and if you're having sex, it's supposed to make you go faster.' (14-year-old girl).

- Enjoyable effects: an instantaneous 'rush', caused by dilating blood vessels and faster heartbeat.

- Duration: around 2 minutes.

- The down side:

  Unpleasant side-effects include headaches, vomiting and dermatitis.

Depressants

Heroin

- Other names: H, smack, junk, scag, gear, brown.

- Heroin is an opiate, derived from the opium poppy. Its close relative, opium, has been used by different societies throughout history. It was easily available in Britain during the 1800s and frequently used by rich and poor alike, as an escape from pain, worry, or drudgery, or simply as a pleasurable pastime.

Heroin is most commonly available as a light brown powder, which is injected, sniffed or smoked. Smoking heroin is known as 'chasing the dragon', and this involves heating the powder on tin foil and inhaling the fumes through a tube of rolled-up foil. Street heroin is frequently cut with other substances and sold in plastic bags or 'wraps' for between £10 and £20 each.

- The up side: 'Heroin brings on a kind of euphoria...it makes me feel comfortable and warm and I feel good about myself. It sometimes helps me forget if there's something I'm upset about.' (29-year-old male).

- Enjoyable effects: creates sensations of warmth and wellbeing; all worries and pain melt away; may induce sleep.

- Duration: approximately 8 hours.

- The down side:

  Heroin users run a high risk of becoming physically and psychologically dependent on the drug and tolerance (needing to take increasing amounts just to feel normal) is inevitable. However, this may take several weeks or months of heavy, regular use.

  First-time users often suffer nausea and vomiting as immediate side-effects.

  The risk of overdose is high, as the user cannot be sure of the amount of pure heroin in his or her 'wrap'.

  For the same reason (as with amphetamine or any other injected drug), injecting can be extremely dangerous and may cause irreversable damage to veins and internal organs.

  Sharing needles carries the risk of HIV, Hepatitis B and blood poisoning.

Regular users may suffer from constipation, malnutrition and for women, the menstrual cycle may become irregular, or stop altogether.

Withdrawal is not dangerous, but is extremely unpleasant, causing severe flu-like symptoms, cramps, nausea and profound mental distress. These symptoms are at their worst for two or three days and gradually fade over the next week or two. Heroin users say the worst problem with withdrawal is fighting their psychological dependence on the drug.

Tranquillisers and sedatives

- Other names: tranx, eggs, jellies, bens, benzos.

- Tranquillisers and sedatives come in many varieties and are prescribed to alleviate anxiety and insomnia. These are meant to be used only for a few weeks, as a coping mechanism during a crisis, but in fact there are more than 250,000 people in the UK who have regular, legal prescriptions - many stretching over periods of several years.

  Tranquillisers most commonly used for recreational purposes (mainly to counteract the effects of stimulants) are benzodiazepenes such as diazepam (Valium), chlordiazepoxide (Librium) and Temazepam, which has recently been withdrawn in Britain in gelatine capsule form, due to the risks associated with injecting it (see below). These drugs are commonly found in medicine cabinets in pill or capsule form, and are available on the street for around £1 for four tablets.

- The up side: 'I get my jellies in 10s or 20s - that's how the dealers sell them. No way would I inject - I swallow them. Jellies make you feel weird. It's a bit like smoking hash - you just sit there and can't move or do a thing.' (14-year-old boy).

- Enjoyable effects: in the short-term, they will have a calming effect and aid sleep.

- Duration: several hours.

- The down side:

  Regular use for more than a few months can result in dependency, depression and aggressive and unpredictable behaviour.

  Mixing these drugs with alcohol is particularly dangerous and can result in overdose and death.

  Injecting Temazepam from dissolved 'jelly' capsules is particularly dangerous, as the substance can resolidify in the body and cause serious problems such as abscesses, thrombosis and gangrene. As with all injected drugs, the risks of serious infection also apply.

  Withdrawal causes unpleasant symptoms such as anxiety, confusion and irritability. Long-term users who want to stop are advised to go through a planned withdrawal programme.

Hallucinogens

Cannabis

- Other names: dope, hash, blow, weed, grass, shit, gear, puff, spliff.

- Cannabis is a mild hallucinogen and by far the most popular illegal drug in the UK today. An extract of the hemp plant, which grows throughout the world, it has been used recreationally in Europe for over a thousand years, but its properties for inducing sleep, stimulating appetite and relieving pain, have been made use of in the East for many thousands of years. The debate is still ongoing as to whether or not the drug should be legalised.

  Cannabis comes in three forms: marijuana (grass), which is

the dried leaves and flowering tops of the female plant; cannabis resin, a brown substance scraped off the stem and pressed into a solid mass, and cannabis oil, which is refined from either the resin or the plant itself. The drug's most active ingredient is a chemical known as THC. Different types of cannabis contain different levels of THC, and due to better cultivation methods, the THC content of today's cannabis is far higher than the amount found in the drug during the 60s.

The most popular way of taking cannabis in all its forms is to smoke it, usually mixed with tobacco, in a 'spliff' made from rolled up cigarette papers and a cardboard tip, or roach. It can also be mixed with food and eaten. Cannabis is grown illegally in the UK, and is also imported from Holland, Central America, Africa and the Middle and Far East. It costs around £25 for a quarter of an ounce, which makes up to 20 spliffs.

- The up side: 'Cannabis gives me a good, drowsy feeling. I sit around and feel that I'm growing out of the ground. Sometimes if I've smoked a lot I see different colours and if I'm listening to music it sounds ace.' (13-year-old boy).

- Enjoyable effects: can be both relaxing and stimulating; users feel sociable, happy; stimulates the appetite; larger quantities or stronger strains may cause hallucinations.

- Duration: the effects of one spliff may last 2-3 hours.

- The down side:

  Cannabis is not known to be physically addictive, but psychological dependence - needing the drug to feel more at ease socially - can occur.

  Cannabis will often enhance the mood of the user and can therefore increase existing feelings of depression or anxiety.

  Because it reduces concentration and affects co-ordination, it should not be used when driving or operating machinery - and it is important to know that it can be detectable in the bloodstream for up to three days.

Rare physical side-effects include rapid heart beat, anxiety, flashbacks and paranoia.

Research is showing that the drug can affect memory and the ability to learn new information.

Users run a higher risk of having accidents while under the influence.

The increasing strength of today's cannabis is giving rise to concern about its physical side-effects.

Smoking cannabis is 27 times more likely to cause lung cancer than smoking a legal cigarette.

After heavy use, individuals may experience anxiety, irritability and sleeplessness.

LSD (Lysergic Acid Diethylamide)

- Other names: acid, trips.

- LSD was first manufactured in the USA during the 1940s, as an experimental drug used by the CIA to rehabilitate victims of brainwashing, and by psychiatrists to attempt to treat patients. The drug was popular during the 50s among musicians and writers, who believed it enhanced their creativity, but its influence became widespread during the 60s, when it reached Britain on a wave of psychedelia, which changed the music and fashion industries forever and opened a new and colourful perspective on the world for young people. Many music historians argue that without LSD, the psychedelic era would never have existed.

Acid comes in the form of illegally-manufactured 'tabs' - small squares of blotting paper, printed with various transfer-style designs, such as strawberries, abstract shapes, and cartoon characters. These are dissolved on the tongue. Each tab costs around £4.

- The up side: 'It takes about half an hour to have any effect, then your mind goes into a different place. I once thought I was being chased by Mars Bars carrying knives and forks.' (14-year-old girl).

- Enjoyable effects: after half an hour or so, colours appear sharper, moving patterns can be seen and moving objects leave traces behind them; later, amazing visions may appear; time seems to stand still and the user can think he/she is in an entirely different world.

- Duration: may last up to 12 hours.

- The down side:

  LSD does not cause either psychological or physical dependence and there is no evidence of long-term damage to the body, and little evidence of long-term damage to personality or behaviour. However, a bad LSD trip can cause nightmarish hallucinations and induce paranoia, terror and anxiety, and it is not advisable to take the drug if you are feeling angry or upset.

  It is also possible that the drug could trigger psychotic behaviour in someone with diagnosed or latent mental illness.

  It's important that the drug is taken in a safe place, as hallucinations can distort judgement and may lead to serious accidents in areas where there are safety hazards.

  Unexpected 'flashbacks' (re-experiencing the effects of a trip) may also occur at a time when no LSD has been taken.

Liberty Cap Mushrooms

- Other names: magic mushrooms, mushies.

- Magic mushrooms have grown wild in Britain for thousands of years, their hallucinogenic powers used to create mystical experiences during ancient religious rituals. They can be found in damp grassy areas between September and November and are used today as a natural (and cheap) alternative to LSD.

The mushrooms, which contain the drug psilocybin, can be eaten raw or cooked, and dried mushrooms are often made into a tea. Users will pick the mushrooms themselves, or buy them dried for a few pounds.

- The up side: 'I've picked and eaten mushies a few times. They're easy enough to find. They have the same effects as trips (LSD), but they don't last as long.' (13-year-old boy).

- Enjoyable effects: between 20 and 30 mushrooms will create a powerful trip, with sensations and hallucinations very similar to those produced by LSD.

- Duration: around 4 hours.

- The down side:

  The white Liberty Cap mushroom is similar to poisonous varieties, and dangerous mistakes can be made.

  The correct variety may still cause stomach pains and diarrhoea.

Solvents

Glue, aerosols, correction fluid, marker pens, petrol and lighter fuel

- Other names: gas

- Solvents are normally classified separately from other drugs, and may have both stimulant and hallucinatory effects. These are most commonly used by young people (between 6% and 9% of school age children have tried them), and are regarded by many health experts as among the most dangerous types of drugs, as they can cause serious illness - even death - the very first time they are used.

Users can be categorised as: experimental sniffers (try once or twice and then stop); regular sniffers (who go through a phase lasting several months and then stop), and long-term users (young people who tend to have problems in their lives, and find solvents help them to cope).

- The up side: 'Glue is for glue-pots...nutters. I've taken gas a few times, though. It makes me feel like a zombie. One time a Ninja turtle came and spoke to me.' (13-year-old boy).

  'I took gas with my mate once and it was a good laugh. We both fell down and didn't even know we'd fallen until later.'(14-year-old girl).

- Enjoyable effects: can be similar to those produced by alcohol; causes an instant euphoric rush; may also induce hallucinations.

- Duration: a few minutes.

- The down side:

  More than 120 young people a year die as a direct result of using solvents.

  Sniffing can cause heart failure, and spraying aerosols into the mouth can freeze the throat and cause suffocation.

  Users also run the risk of suffocating if they are sniffing from plastic bags.

  Intoxication can cause some youngsters to do dangerous things.

Alcohol

- Other names: booze, drink, liquor.

- Alcohol is a depressant drug which slows down both physical and mental reactions. It has always been popular in the UK and is more commonly used today than ever before. It is widely available in supermarkets, off-licenses, licensed premises and most domestic homes, and is used by people of all ages for a variety of reasons, such as helping them to relax, have fun, forget their worries, lose their inhibitions, and overcome fear or pain. Alcohol ranges in price, but, for example, a beer-drinking man sticking to the government's safe ceiling of 3-4 units a day may spend up to £30 a week on his own alcohol consumption.

- The up side: 'Drink makes me feel happy. It stops me feeling shy or nervous. I drink with my friends and we have a laugh.'(15-year-old girl).

- The down side:

  Alcohol can cause aggressive and violent behaviour, serious accidents, unsafe sex, poor foetal development during pregnancy, death due to choking on vomit, or overdose caused by mixing alcohol with other drugs.

  Long-term heavy use leads to physical dependence and tolerance, and may damage the heart, liver, stomach and brain.

  Every year in the UK, around 30,000 deaths are attributed to alcohol.

Nicotine

- Other names: cigarettes, cigars, fags, ciggies, smokes.

- Nicotine, found in tobacco leaves, is a stimulant drug which increases pulse rate and blood pressure. Tobacco has been widely used in the UK since the early 1600s and smoking has followed numerous fashion trends ever since.

  During the 'age of innocence' before the full effects of tobacco were realised, cigarettes reached their peak of popularity in the 1940s, when smoking was glamorised by Hollywood movie stars of both sexes.

  Today, smoking tends to be seen as a bad habit, rather than an attraction - except, perhaps, by many young people (girls, especially), who still believe it enhances their image. On average, a pack of 20 cigarettes costs £2.80 - £3.00.

- The up side: 'If I smoke, I feel better - not so worried about things.' (16-year-old girl).

- Enjoyable effects: helps regular users feel more relaxed and better able to concentrate.

- Duration: the effects of one cigarette can last up to 30 minutes.

- The down side:

  Stopping smoking can cause restlessness, irritability and depression.

  Chest and breathing problems are common among smokers.

  Long-term users run a greater risk of developing lung cancer, heart disease, circulatory problems and ulcers.

  Smoking during pregnancy can cause foetal damage.

  Passive smoking can damage the health of non-smokers, and may cause babies and small children in particular to develop chest problems.

Every year in the UK, more than 111,000 people die from smoking-related diseases.

- Many drug users may use a range of drugs to enhance or counteract each other's effects, eg someone taking a stimulant such as ecstasy or speed may later take a tranquilliser, or smoke some cannabis, to 'bring them down', so that they can sleep. Dealers will often sell 'party bags' of mixed drugs, for this purpose.

Summing up...

Well done! You've negotiated your way through the thorny tangle of all the different drugs and their various effects, and you've found out the sobering facts about alcohol and smoking, and how they compare with illicit drugs. It's likely you've made many interesting discoveries, which you'll want to think about and discuss with others - including, hopefully, your child.

Most people, when they read about drugs, find themselves fascinated by the subject - so is it any wonder that certain youngsters should want to try them out for themselves? Let's meet some of these young people and find out why they have chosen to experiment with different types of illicit drugs.

4 DOING DRUGS

- Why do it?
- Young drug users talking
- Summing up...

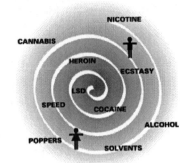

Why do it?

Having looked at all the different types of drugs, and discovered the risks attached, it's natural enough to wonder why young people take drugs in the first place. As we saw in Chapter Two, the answer to this is by no means straightforward.

Just think about why we all use drugs in one form or another. Why do we persist in drinking coffee, tea or alcohol; smoking; depending on prescribed drugs, and eating sugary and salty foods, when we know they carry risks to our health and/or social life? Well, we do these things for a variety of reasons:

- to control stress, anxiety, nervousness, loneliness, or pain
- to help us relax
- to fill in time
- to be sociable and socially acceptable

- because it's part of our culture
- to give us a buzz
- to make life more interesting or exciting
- to attract attention
- to rebel
- because they make us feel good

Youngsters may take drugs for any or all of these reasons. They may be having problems at home or at school - or they may simply be curious to try something they see as different, forbidden or exciting.

Young drug users talking

It's all very well to theorise, but the best way of finding out is to ask the drug users themselves. In the next few pages, young people from different social backgrounds, explain in their own words the attraction drugs hold for them...

- 'I started taking drugs when I was 11 because all my mates were doing it and we were bored. I've taken hash, speed, jellies, gas, acid, mushies...but I would never take heroin. There are heaps of dealers at school. They get the drugs from their dealers, further up the ladder.

  'I probably like hash and speed the best. They make me feel ace. I've had bad trips before. One time, on acid, I didn't know where I was and it was scary...another time I took a few jellies and suddenly I was two miles away from where I'd been and I didn't know how I'd got there.

'I've been drunk as well, but it did my head in. I lay at the edge of the river and got soaked and when I got home, I fell over the bin and knocked myself unconscious. I'm not really worried about what drugs do to you, but when I get older I'm only going to smoke hash.' Gordon (13).

- 'I started smoking cannabis when I was 12. I don't think I was pressurised into doing it. A couple of friends did it and I just joined in - they didn't force me, or anything. I still smoke and I enjoy it. It makes me feel relaxed and it's far better for you than cigarettes or alcohol.

  'I think it's rubbish that cannabis leads on to harder drugs - statistics show there are millions of people using cannabis, but only a tiny amount go on to take heroin. I've tried speed once or twice, but that's all, and I've no intention of taking anything else.' Ruth (16)

- 'I've taken lots of different kinds of drugs - poppers, gas, hash, trips, speed. Me and my mates do it for a laugh. I had a scare with speed, though. My mum had to take me to hospital one night after I'd taken it, because I was hitting my head off the walls and wouldn't stop being sick. They took tests at the hospital and told my mum I'd been taking speed. She went mental. She said if I did it again, I wasn't her kid. I've not taken it since, but I still do hash and trips.' Julie (14).

- 'I don't take drugs now, but I did for a while...hash, speed and alcohol. I think I did it because there was nothing else to do except stay in and watch TV.' Simon (15)

- 'My real dad takes drugs - he grows cannabis plants in the lobby. My cousin takes drugs, too. I've taken hash, speed, gas, poppers, E, trips...they're easy enough to get hold of. At school, a fag will cost 30p and a joint costs £2.50. I read a magazine about E and the side-effects and it worried me a bit, but I can't remember what it said now. Nobody my age takes smack - it's bad news.

'My mum says she'll disown me if I take any more drugs, but I know she used to sniff glue when she was a Mod. I've found some good places to hide my speed - in the thick sole of my trainers. But you've got to be careful - I once stood in a puddle and all the speed dissolved.' Andy (14).

- 'I was quite shy when I was at school. I found it difficult to talk to boys and so I never really had a boyfriend. I knew people who took drugs - mostly hash and speed - but I wasn't part of that crowd at all. I used to get depressed, just sitting at home every night. Everyone except me seemed to be having fun.

'I left school with good exam results, but I didn't want to go to university. I didn't know what I wanted to do, but my mum persuaded me to apply for a job in a bank and I got it. The work was boring, but I enjoyed the social life. I met Phil on a night out and we started going steady after that.

'He's three years older than me and he has loads of friends from university who are pretty wild. My mum got quite angry when I started staying out late and there were lots of rows. Well, the upshot was, I moved in with Phil, who rents a flat in the town. Mum was furious and didn't talk to me for a while, but she actually quite likes Phil and after a few weeks, she got used to the idea and things were reasonably okay between us.

'We had a brilliant time in the flat to start with...we'd go to clubs and have parties afterwards. I knew from the start Phil and his friends were into drugs. They'd take things like speed or E before going out -whichever they could get more easily - and then later, they'd puff (smoke cannabis) to help them come down. I was too scared to join in at first. I didn't know anything about drugs except that they were supposed to be bad for you. But everyone seemed to have such an ace time and nobody got really ill or anything, so I started taking stuff, too.

'The difference it made to my confidence was amazing. E and speed give you this fantastic rush...and the energy...it's like you've become Superwoman or something! With E, you're in love with the whole world. Taking E with my friends gives me the best feeling ever. And then, when we're puffing, we have such a laugh...any little thing triggers us off. We're usually starving after that and end up eating loads of chocolate biscuits and crisps at four in the morning.

'The great thing is, you don't need to drink - I wouldn't anyway, on E or speed, because that's dangerous - and you don't really get a hangover, although you can feel pretty low. Phil and I usually fall into bed and sleep for hours after a good night out.

'That's how I lost my job, actually. I mean, we didn't really go out a lot during the week, but after a weekend session, we'd find it really hard to get to sleep for nights afterwards. People were always coming round as well, and we'd end up staying up pretty late and so often I'd be late for work. I was warned a couple of times, but I didn't really care. I'd far rather be enjoying myself and having a social life than going to bed early like a good little bank clerk! So they sacked me. That was about four months ago.

'Mum went mad, of course. I didn't tell her at first, but she soon found out. I told her why they'd sacked me, but she didn't understand. I don't blame her, really, because she doesn't know I take drugs and she said I never slept in when I was living at home.

'The worst part of it is having no money. With Phil being a student, it was mostly my money we lived on, and now I've no income, we're broke all the time. Some days, when he's at university, I'll stay in bed until late afternoon. There's not much point in getting up. I feel down a lot of the time. It's not the drugs...they make me happy. The only problem with them is the cost.' Janice (18).

- 'I was a heroin user - smoking and injecting - for about six years. I'm now on a methadone programme and I get my methadone once a day. I'm not ready to come off yet...I want to keep things just as they are right now.

'I was 12 when I started taking drugs...smoking a joint behind the bike sheds, that sort of thing. It was something to do. Then I tried speed and poppers and went on to temgesics, codeine...tablet painkillers. I started injecting them when I was 18 - I got someone to do the first injection for me.

'I was about 23 when I first used heroin. There was a group of us, we all tried it together. The first time, I puked up all night. I didn't try it again until six months later. After a few times, I started to enjoy it. It gives you a warm, comfortable feeling. One of the guys who was there the first time I tried it was only 13. He didn't do any more until years later, but he got hooked eventually. He died a year ago, of a brain haemorrhage. Two of my mates have died from overdoses in the last couple of weeks.

'Heroin is much easier to get nowadays. It comes from all over - Glasgow, Liverpool, London. By the time it comes up to Aberdeen, it's been cut with all the shit of the day. So when you do get pure H, it's easy to OD (overdose). Someone OD'd in my house the other week. I slapped him and rubbed his face and got him out of it. A couple of days before that, someone OD'd in another mate's house and he dragged him outside and right away from the house... he didn't want to know. I couldn't do that. I would get a doctor or an ambulance to the house. I know about first aid and what to do.

'I hid my habit from my mother for years. She thought I was just smoking hash. The doctor came in one morning to see her. He knew about me and I was fed up keeping it secret, so I asked him to tell her the truth. She was great, really. She couldn't believe I'd hidden it from her for so long, but she said she'd rather know than not. She's been really supportive.

'It wouldn't have been any use if she'd gone mad and stopped me going out. Nothing would have stopped me. When you're a heroin user, your mind is racing all the time, thinking of how you're going to get your next fix. You can't sleep or anything. It takes up a big part of your life.

'I got busted a year ago for buying heroin off a 'mate'. The bastard set me up. I was charged and given a £50 fine - only because I'd never had a record before that.

'Methadone is worse than heroin, I think. Coming off is murder - months later, you're still not sleeping well, you've still got all the physical and psychological hurts...stomach cramps and that. Tranquillisers are the same.

'If I had kids I'd wouldn't want them to do what I've done. What worries me is that a lot of folk now have started smoking heroin, to bring themselves down from taking speed or E. We used to smoke hash or take jellies. Another scary thing is crack - you're starting to see it on the street now, and it's really bad news...the big time.' Gordon (29).

Summing up...

These stories, frightening though they may be, are not deliberately sensational. They simply reflect the realities of drug-taking today. For some of these young people, trying drugs is a phase they will grow out of; others may carry on, but lead perfectly normal lives, and yet others may find their drug taking increasingly difficult to cope with as it begins to bring them serious health and social problems. The range of outcomes, like the range of reasons for taking drugs, will vary enormously.

What is important here is to face up to the fact that drug-taking, for many young people, is part of growing up. This does not mean every youngster is doing it, or that everyone who tries it will end up hooked on heroin. But there are thousands out there who are experimenting with all kinds of drugs.

All of us will remember experimenting with various new experiences during our teens - think of smoking, drinking, staying out all night, sex, fooling around with ouija boards, fast driving, to name but a few.

It's a frightening thought for parents that their children are going to do similar, or more worrying, things. But there is simply no way adults can prevent young people from experimenting with life.

What we can do, however, is help educate children about the realities of life by acknowledging the highs, pointing out the dangers, and ensuring that they know they can always confide in us, no matter what happens.

So how can we best put this into practice? The two key words are education and communication - and we'll look at these in the next two chapters.

- Bear in mind that most of us rely on drugs in one form or another.

- Think about your own reasons for smoking/drinking alcohol, tea or coffee/taking tranquillisers or painkillers.

- Try to keep an open mind about why young people may use drugs.

- Consider using some of the young people's stories featured in this chapter when you talk to your child about drugs.

5 TALKING DRUGS

- Education networks
- What's happening?
- Start talking!
- Summing up...

'There are very strong arguments for not using drugs. Unfortunately, up to now, society hasn't articulated them very well.'

This comment from a senior police officer involved in drugs education acknowledges the widespread confusion about drugs, which has done little to equip young people for life in a drug-taking society.

To a great extent, drugs have been uninvited guests, catching us unawares and moving in with all their baggage before we've realised they're here to stay. This has happened so quickly that it has taken time for us to latch on to the problem and develop what is generally agreed as the best means, along with law enforcement, of addressing it: drugs education. As a result, we are only now beginning to pass on the information and skills vital to today's youngsters.

It's very tempting for parents who know little about the subject to leave drugs education to schools. But, as teachers and anyone else involved in education will tell you, parents are in fact the best educators of their children, as they have the most influence from the very beginning of a child's life.

Education Networks

Education of any kind works best if it is delivered consistently throughout society, ie by nurseries, schools, colleges, universities, libraries, churches and other religious organisations, health authorities, toy and games manufacturers, community initiatives, charities, police, voluntary services and all forms of the media. Parents and other members of the family play a major part in this network, reinforcing (or redefining, since it's not a perfect world!) what children are learning from these influences, and showing how it can relate specifically to them.

Drugs education, despite its relatively slow start, is now beginning to work in the same way. A vast network of national and independent agencies and organisations, including and in addition to those mentioned above, is steadily developing to spread accurate information about drugs and drugs issues (many also provide support for drug users and their families - see Help List, pages 101-103). And again, as a parent, your contribution to this is vital. By reading this book, you are taking the first step towards helping to educate your child about drugs. But there are many more ways in which you can become involved.

What's Happening?

The next step is to find out what is happening in your area. To help you, here's a brief roundup of the types of drug education initiatives which may be going on around you. Any of the following agencies will be more than happy to bring you up to date with their drug education activities. For details on how to contact them, see Help List, pages 101-103.

Schools

In line with the Government's National Curriculum document, schools throughout the UK are at varying stages of integrating drug education programmes into the curriculum. These are beginning to be introduced at primary level, as it is now understood that by the time they reach secondary school, many children already have some knowledge of drugs, gleaned from such sources as older brothers and sisters and television programmes, which may not be well-informed.

A wide variety of programmes exist, many of them pilots set up by schools in conjunction with other local agencies. For example, these may involve differing degrees of input from health promotion workers, community police officers, drug workers, former drug users and other young people specially trained to talked to their peers about drugs. They may also take the form of role-play workshops, debates, exhibitions and a variety of other creative projects.

But however they are implemented, all of these

programmes share the common aims of both improving young people's knowledge of drug facts and helping to raise their self-esteem, so that they can make informed (and hopefully healthy) choices when faced with situations involving drugs.

Many schools are now closely involving parents in their drug education programmes. Some are holding drug awareness evenings for parents, which, again, may include other agencies such as support groups, community police and health education agencies. Others, within the context of the curriculum, are encouraging youngsters to ask questions at home about drugs, eg some primary schools task children to follow up lessons on prescription medicines by asking them to ask their parents about their own medicine cabinets. In this way, drug messages such as the dangers of certain drugs, why they are taken, etc, can be reinforced by the parents in ways which are familiar and specific to each individual child.

Other school initiatives involve running mini-courses for parents, covering areas such as effective communication skills or helping children learn outside the school environment, and organising group discussions on drug education and how parents can help.

Many schools are also formulating policies on how to deal with drug-taking or drug-dealing in school (see Chapter Seven), and they are taking steps to inform parents of what they are doing and why.

All in all, schools are undoubtedly playing a pioneering role in drug education - but to do this effectively they need the support of parents.

Colleges & Universities

Further and higher education are helping to reinforce drugs messages through such initiatives as start-of-term health fairs, ongoing health information and advice, and student counselling support.

Health Authorities

Government health education bodies the Health Education Authority (HEA) and the Health Education Board for Scotland (HEBS) provide a plethora of drugs information and advice for the general public, health professionals, drugs agencies, workplaces and anyone involved in education, in the form of publications, posters, videos, promotional launches and high-profile media campaigns. Materials - many of them targeting parents - are widely available, either directly, or from health centres, local health authorities, drug agencies and voluntary organisations.

The health promotion divisions of local health authorities throughout the UK are involved in a diverse range of drugs education activities, working in partnership with schools, parents, private enterprise, police forces, local authorities and voluntary organisations, to provide young people and adults with consistent messages about drugs.

Drugs Prevention Initiative

In England, the government-led DPI involves 12 local drugs prevention teams working with their communities to develop effective ways of preventing the spread of drug use.

Drugs Services

A complex network of government, local authority and independent drug services exists throughout the UK, providing general drugs information and advice, as well as support for drug users and their families and friends.

Community Education

Drugs education is central to most community education programmes, and there are literally hundreds of projects in operation throughout the UK. These involve community-led activities ranging from after-school clubs and outreach projects teaching drug users about harm minimisation, to video-making workshops and courses in assertiveness and stress-handling.

Voluntary Organisations

Again, there are hundreds of voluntary organisations providing information, support and advice relating to drugs.

Police

Each police force has an active community education division, which involves community police officers working in partnership with local health and education authorities and a range of other agencies, to provide accurate information about drugs.

Start Talking!

The very first piece of advice each one of these organisations will give to you as a parent is to start (or continue) talking to your child about drugs. And to do this meaningfully, you need to find out how much he or she already knows about them.

If this sounds daunting, don't worry. In the next chapter we'll look at how you can broach the subject and keep the lines of communication open. But first, let's see what youngsters and parents think about drugs education, and how they feel about talking to each other about drugs.

Young people

- 'I think we should respect our parents' experience. They're not aliens - they've gone through adolescence themselves, and we should be able to learn from them.' Anna

- 'I wouldn't talk to my parents about drugs - I'd find it embarrassing and so would they. I'd rather talk to my friends.' Lucy

- 'Our parents were young in the 60s and 70s, when the whole drugs thing came on the scene. It's silly to think they don't understand, because they must have been through it all themselves.' Paul

- 'We don't want health experts or police telling us about drugs - we want young people who have been through drug experiences themselves coming into schools and telling us the truth about what it's like.' Avril

- 'We need a society where the barriers are down and adults

and kids can talk. Parents think drugs equal death and kids think drugs equal fun. Parents need to recognise the good side, and kids need to recognise the bad side. A lot of people are taking drugs and having fun, and are not addicts.' Beverley

Parents

- 'I need to know everything I can about drugs. I've had no contact with them throughout my life - I'm 35 and I've never seen any. I want to be able to educate my children - they're 12, 10 and six. I have spoken to them already about drugs - basically telling them they're something they shouldn't be touching, as they can ruin your life. So far, they've listened and seem to have accepted that, but it's time to take things a bit further, especially since my eldest is now at secondary school' Arlene

- 'One of the main things I need to know is how to recognise the symptoms of drug use and what to do if I find my children are taking drugs.' Jonathon

- 'I would like to know more about the different kinds of drugs and what they do. I'm a single parent with girls of 13, 17 and 19, and I find it quite easy to talk to them about drugs, although I don't know much about them at all. We've always been very close and it's not an embarrassing subject.' Maureen

- 'Drugs are being discussed at primary school now, but a lot of parents don't want to know. How can drugs education work if the parents won't take the issue on board? We need to have more young people who have taken drugs going into the schools to tell kids what it's really like. Someone I know lost her brother through septicaemia, brought on by injecting drugs, and she told me later she wished she had been able to take a video camera to the hospital, so that she could show other young people how he had died.' Karen

- 'I smoke hash to help me relax. I've got four kids and the oldest is 11. I wouldn't be happy about my kids taking drugs. Hash is different. I don't want them to take it, but I'd rather it was hash than anything else. My oldest son, he's just started secondary school and he's not stupid. He knows a lot more about drugs than I ever did at that age. I think he found out about them from his friends.

  'I've asked him if he takes any, but he always says no. My younger kids haven't got a clue about drugs and I don't really want them to know. I've never smoked hash in front of my kids. If I did, my eldest would have it all round the neighbourhood in five minutes. He does suspect something, because he'll walk into the living room and sniff the air. He must smell the smoke. He never says anything, though.'
  Sandra

- 'Annie, my little girl, is three and I smoke hash in front of her. She knows not to touch my special fags. To her, they're just cigarettes. I think things like mushies and acid are just as bad as heroin, with all the flashbacks you can get. They're pretty freaky. I'd far rather my daughter came in smoking hash than smoking fags. When she gets older, I'm going to talk to her about drugs and be honest about my own drug taking.' Viv

- 'I would love to be able to talk to my teenage kids about drugs, but they just won't have it. As soon as I start to broach the subject of drugs, or sex, they just roll their eyes and say 'you don't have a clue'.

  'They seem to know it all already, but what worries me is that I don't know what they're up to. They certainly wouldn't come and tell me if they were taking drugs. My daughter didn't even tell me when she started her periods! I was really hurt about that, because I thought she'd want to share that with me, but she couldn't see why I was so upset. 'Get a life, Mum', is all she and her brother ever say.

'I like to think I'm a good listener and I'd love us to communicate more, but they're just not the kind of kids who like to sit around and discuss things.' Rita

- 'I've always tried to act on my belief that I should trust and respect my son as an equal human being, and not try to control him or keep things from him. It's not always easy - lots of times you want to tell kids what to do or what to think, or just tell them to shut up and leave you in peace!

'My son is 10 now, and he knows I love him and that we can speak about anything at all. I'm under no illusions that he'll want to experiment with drugs when he's older and I have to respect that, too. I trust him to make the right decisions, but if he gets in any trouble, he knows he can come to me.' Lindsay

- 'We have two boys of 17 and 15 and they're like chalk and cheese when it comes to communicating.

'Our elder son will talk to us about most things - he likes to chat about what he and his friends have been doing, and his friends will come round to the house a lot. Most of the time, they'll sit in the kitchen talking. We don't mind - we'd rather that than not know where he is or what he's up to. He's quite open about what goes on at parties - we know most of the kids drink, including our son, and that some do smoke cannabis (he says he doesn't).

'The younger boy, on the other hand, tells us nothing. He never brings his friends home, and we don't know who they are. We know he smokes and probably drinks at parties, but he thinks we're not aware of that. We just have to hope that he's not taking drugs - there's certainly been no sign of it. As I smoke, I can't very well tell him not to, but I do tell him it's not worth it. He's never come home in a state, and he knows the facts about using condoms, etc, so we just have to hope he's sensible enough not to get into trouble.' Robert

Summing up...

The main message coming through for parents is to start talking to their children about drugs - and the earlier the better. But many parents find it hard to communicate with their children at all, especially if they are going through adolescence. As one parent puts it: 'How do you start a meaningful conversation with someone who looks daggers at you if you so much as ask them to pass the salt?'

It would be all very well to smugly announce that if you had put good parenting and communication skills into practice at an early stage, you would already have a strong enough relationship with your child so that he or she would feel happy to share their innermost secrets with you while growing up.

But this is the real world, and there is no such thing as the perfect parent. You may now regret not investing enough time in communicating with your child in the past - but that is in the past. Let it go. Remember that there are many positive steps you can take to improve your relationship in the present and future, and the next chapter will help you make a start.

Alternatively, you may feel that you have built up a close, trusting relationship with your child over the years, but that it doesn't seem to be helping at this stage in their lives. It's natural to feel disappointed and let down if you feel they are rejecting years of love, trust and friendship by no longer sharing the details of their lives. But it's also natural for young people to withdraw from their parents while they build their own world, with friends taking centre stage.

- In each case, the most important thing you can do is try to keep talking to each other. And here's where you start.

- Always remember that you as a parent have an enormous influence in educating your child.

- Make an effort to find out what kind of drug education initiatives are happening in your area and where you can get more information and support if you need it.

- Ask your child's school how you can help continue their drugs education at home.

- If the school is not yet involved in drug education, ask why not!

6 KEEP TALKING – PRACTICAL COMMUNICATION SKILLS

- So what is good communication?
- Listening and observing
- Active listening
- Talking
- Getting started
- Summing up...

Most of us are probably aware that good communication helps to build close, trusting relationships, and that poor communication can lead to misunderstandings and alienation from others. But how many of us are good at putting good communication into practice?

In this chapter, we concentrate on face-to-face communication, looking at ways in which we can improve our own skills and at the same time encourage others - not just children and teenagers - to respond positively to our efforts. These skills are valuable tools which can be applied in any situation where good communication is important, for instance when talking meaningfully to our partners, family, friends or colleagues.

So what is 'good communication'?

Good face-to-face communication is as much about listening and observing as it is about talking.

Think of someone you know who likes to talk, but not to listen. How do you feel when you try to tell them something and they dismiss it by either changing the subject, or by 'hi-jacking' the topic and relating it to their own experience?

That's right, you feel rejected. You realise this is not a two-way conversation at all, that you're being used simply as a sounding board by a selfish person who probably knows little or nothing about you. It's not a pleasant experience.

But if we're really honest with ourselves, aren't we all a little guilty of not listening at times?

There are many distractions in our lives which prevent us from taking time to really listen to what even those closest to us are trying to tell us. We talk at each other across a cacophony of white noise produced by the television, radio, computer games and CD players which dominate our leisure time at home; we exchange hurried messages in the short periods before dashing to work, or over a quick meal before rushing away to evening classes/sports events/ pubs and nightclubs. We are slowly losing the art of really talking and listening to each other.

The good news is that we can do something about it - starting today. Before we tackle talking, let's start by taking a look at the two other closely-related components of good communication - listening and observing.

Listening and observing

In good communication, there should be far more to listening than simply hearing what is being said. We need to understand - and to understand not only what someone is telling us, but also why they are telling us, and if they are telling us what they truly believe. In other words, we need to know where they're coming from.

Life would be far simpler if we all said what we meant. But we don't. There are all kinds of reasons for this, but two of the most important are that we don't want to be vulnerable, and we don't want to hurt those we love. And so, afraid to expose our true feelings, we underplay our emotions, tell half-truths, lie outright, keep our thoughts to ourselves, say the opposite of what we mean...the list is endless!

It's best, then, not always to take what you hear at face value unless you are sure the speaker truly believes what he or she is saying. But how can you tell? That's where observation comes in.

How many times have you wished, during an important telephone conversation, that you could see the speaker - that it would help you understand more clearly where they're coming from? In face-to-face conversation we have the advantage of observing body language.

Many hundreds of books have been written about body language over the years, and it's still by no means a cut and dried subject. Current thinking suggests that if you're trying to understand what someone is really trying to tell you, there's little point in consulting a body language 'dictionary' of typical facial expressions and gestures. These tend to be very general and can be open to misinterpretation.

It's far more helpful for our purposes to remember that, assuming the person we are communicating with is not a stranger, we will know them enough to be able to tell in most cases how they feel about what they are saying. Think about it: you've seen your children or partner reacting to many thousands of different situations over the years - you, probably more than anyone else, will understand their idiosyncratic expressions and gestures. You know when they're feeling unwell, angry, happy, excited, sullen, hopeful, and so on. All you need to do is pay attention, and, to quote an old song, 'listen with your eyes.'

Active Listening

Active listening involves a degree of talking and is one of these skills which is easy enough to understand, but hard to put into practice! It is well worth persevering with, however, as it is especially useful in the case of emotionally difficult conversations.

Basically, active listening helps an important conversation to progress and develop, and hopefully this will lead to mutual understanding. Without active listening, conversations can break down, become inane, or degenerate into arguments, leaving both parties feeling dissatisfied and no further forward in understanding the other's point of view. Active listening involves:

- Setting your own feelings aside and really listening to what you are being told.

- Observing the speaker to see how he/she is feeling.

- Making an effort to understand where he/she is coming from.

- Showing you do understand and are sympathetic - by nodding, using appropriate facial expressions, etc.

- Not being judgmental.

- Not interrupting with solutions, arguments, or indignant remarks.

- Thinking of yourself as a mirror, reflecting back what the other person appears to be feeling and trying to tell you.

Here is an example of how active listening can turn a potentially explosive exchange into a meaningful conversation.

Without active listening

Mother: 'Why aren't you going out tonight, Sheila?'

Teenage daughter (on the verge of tears): 'Danny doesn't want to see me any more. He finished with me this afternoon.'

Mother: 'Never mind, love. There are plenty more fish in the sea. I didn't like that boy anyway - he had no manners and he always seemed to look down on you...(door slams) *Sheila*! Where are you going?'

With active listening

Mother: 'Why aren't you going out tonight, Sheila?'

Teenage daughter (on the verge of tears): 'Danny doesn't want to see me any more. He finished with me this afternoon.'

Mother: 'Oh, love...you're very upset. He means a lot to you, doesn't he?'

Daughter (sobbing): 'I really love him, Mum. I thought he felt the same way. Now I feel he was just using me.'

Mother: 'It's okay to cry, love. It's horrible to feel someone has used you. Will this make things difficult for you in class..?'

As we can see, active listening has helped this conversation progress from a three-second disaster to a longer discussion about how the girl will cope with being rejected by her boyfriend.

Although the mother feels furious with the boy for hurting her daughter, she knows her anger is not important here. What matters is how her daughter is feeling and how she will come to terms with what at any age is a traumatic situation.

Resisting the temptation to judge and give your opinion is extremely difficult. We all like to think we can solve other people's problems and can pontificate for hours about how things should be. But as our example above demonstrates, this is not helpful at all.

If you're asked for your opinion, however, be honest. Take our example above: if the woman's daughter were to ask her if she is angry with the boy, there would be no reason for the mother not to admit that she is indeed angry. But rather than rant on about his bad points, it would be far more beneficial to then ask her daughter if she feels angry too. That could lead to her listing all his bad points, and perhaps realising for herself that he is not worth all the upset. Human nature being what it is, if she hears herself say it, rather than her mother telling her, she is more inclined to believe it!

Hopefully, this conversation will have brought mother and daughter closer together and laid the foundations for other important discussions in the future.

Talking

As we've seen, good listening skills can help make talking easier. Active listening will usually prompt a response, from which you in turn can take your cue. It may be slow, hard or even painful, but you will find that eventually you will reach a point where you are getting to the heart of the matter and are truly communicating with each other.

But all this begs the question that you're engaged in conversation in the first place. We've ignored what can often be the biggest stumbling block of all - getting started.

Initiating an important conversation may be nerve-wracking, awkward or embarrassing, if you're not confident about how to go about it. Supposing the person you are addressing becomes scornful, hostile or defensive? What if it develops into a full-scale row? 'Getting heavy' is often a daunting prospect and it's easy to see why we can all at times find better things to do than broach a difficult subject!

Getting Started

As we've seen in Chapter Five, the first step towards effective communication about drugs is to find out how much your child knows. This example suggests a way of broaching the subject of drugs in order to do this. It's by no means a formula which should be followed to the letter (if only it was that easy!) You may not believe it at the moment, but you are the one who knows best how to talk to your child. Just remember to listen, observe and respond in a way which encourages further conversation.

- First of all, choose your moment. This in itself is a tricky task, as many families spend much of the time doing their own thing in separate rooms or outside the home. Try to pick a time when you are not tired or hungry.

  Perhaps this could be after the evening meal (during is not a good idea, as difficult or important conversations have a habit of causing indigestion!), or at a quiet time during the weekend.

- Involve other members of the family if you can - this is a subject to which everyone can contribute, and it makes the conversation less formal and intimidating. Drugs can be discussed in many different contexts, and, unless you want to tackle a particular issue in private (eg if you have reason to believe your child is taking drugs and want to find out if this is true), broaching the subject during a normal family gathering can be beneficial for younger children and grandparents, who may know very little about drugs.

- Introduce the subject as naturally as possible. You might want to use this book as a starting point, eg: 'I've been reading a book on drugs and I had no idea that magic mushrooms can be found all over the country/drugs are so easily available in schools/heroin is not so popular with young people as I'd thought,' etc. Whatever you say, it must be genuine - remember, your child knows you as well as you know him/her and the last thing you want them to think is 'oh-oh - here comes the Spanish Inquisition'.

- Observe the response. If it's sighs and rolling eyes, don't be put off. This could mean that they think either you're out of your depth and they know more than you do, or they think they're in for a lecture. So surprise them - bow to their greater knowledge with, eg: 'Oh, it looks like you know all about drugs - you learn about them at school, don't you? Did you know, though, that...' This challenge to their superior intellect will hopefully be too tempting to ignore and the conversation could then go down many interesting paths. If the reaction is positive and your child volunteers some information, don't be tempted to jump in with such emotive phrases as: 'promise me you'll never take drugs'/'your father would kill you if he found out you were taking drugs,' etc. Remember to practise active listening.

- If you're challenged about your own drug use, ie of painkillers, tranquillisers, alcohol, smoking, don't get defensive. Be honest about why you use them and acknowledge the damage these drugs are causing in society. Again, this could lead into a lively discussion and it may enable you to broach the important issues of health and the law. If the conversation is going well and your child is responding positively, try passing on some of the information you have learned in this book (see Chapters Three and Seven for the health and legal implications of taking drugs). But be prepared to be challenged, as myths about drugs are just as common among young people as they are among adults. This is a good opportunity to hammer a few on the head!

- If you are feeling confident, steer the conversation in a more personal direction. Ask if your child/children know anyone who takes drugs. If they tell you they do, remember not to panic or be judgmental. Listen to what they are saying and try to understand how they are feeling and what they really think about their friends' drug-taking. Do they appear frightened/curious/ashamed/defensive/disgusted/admiring/tolerant? Use active listening to reflect that feeling back. For example, if the child appears to be frightened, why not say: 'You seem to be a bit worried about that. Are they trying to get you to take cannabis too?' Alternatively, if the child seems to admire his/her friend's behaviour, you could say: 'Do you think he's quite brave, then? Do you wish you could do it too?' Seeing that you are not angry or upset may encourage them to confide in you further.

- If the response is extreme embarrassment, hostility or defensiveness and you suspect your child is not just being loyal to his/her friends, again, don't panic. Calmly say: 'This conversation seems to be upsetting you. Is there something worrying you?' This is a good time to let them know that if something is worrying them they can always count on you to be there for them. If they see you are not angry or judgmental, this may encourage them to talk further, but even if they make it obvious that the conversation is over, they will not forget your caring attitude and will know they can broach the subject when they're ready.

- If it does come out that your child is using drugs, you will undoubtedly feel shocked, distressed and out of your depth. The next chapter will help you find the best way of coping with this situation, whether you choose to do this on your own, as a family, or with the help of a support agency.

Summing up...

All these pointers to communicating effectively with your child may lead you in many directions. The first conversation could well pave the way for regular discussions which could turn out to be enjoyable experiences for the whole family.

For the purposes of this book, the subject here has been drugs. But it can't be stressed enough that these techniques could equally apply to discussing any topic under the sun.

Good communication takes practice and patience. It also comes with a degree of responsibility. Once you have opened the door and shown that you can truly listen and understand, you can't just slam it shut when it suits you. You may not always be in the mood to talk when your children/partner want to discuss something, but it's worth making the effort to give them the time they are asking for.

- Building a trusting, loving, communicative relationship is not easy - but it can bring wonderful rewards which will last a lifetime.

- Make sure you understand what good communication is all about.

- Know the benefits of listening and observation.

- Learn the basics of active listening.

- Use our 'Getting Started' guide to help you broach the subject of drugs with your child.

- Remember - these skills will stand you in good stead no matter who you are talking to.

7 DRUGS AND THE LAW

- Case studies
- The facts
- Did you know it is an offence to..?
- Schools drugs policies
- What happens if your child is held for questioning by police?
- Cautions and warnings
- Prosecution
- Summing up...

Case studies

- Eighteen-year-old John landed a job as a driver for a pharmaceutical company. A keen motorist, he was delighted with the job and took pride in his work. A few months later, he was caught in possession of cannabis (only enough for his own use). His court case was covered in the local newspaper. Soon afterwards, his employer sacked him.

- Mary is 16 and uses hallucinogenics. Following a number of visits from the police, her furious parents threw her out of the house. Mary is now a prostitute.

- James (19) is studying languages at college. A year ago, he was convicted for supplying ecstasy. Recently, he has applied for a visa to travel abroad. He has been refused visas for two out of the three countries he wanted to visit.

- Helen was expelled from her fee-paying school for sharing a spliff with two friends. This happened before she was due to sit her Higher Grades. Since then, she has been unable to find another centre in which to sit her exams and now she fears she has lost out on the possibility of further education.

- During his teens, Jack had a number of convictions for possession of various drugs. Now 26, he has been drug and conviction free for eight years. He recently applied for a job which required candidates to declare any previous convictions. Unaware of the implications, he did not declare his. He was offered the job, subject to a check on previous convictions. A few days later, the offer was withdrawn.

As well as being aware of the various health issues connected with drug use, it's important that parents and their children are clear about the legal implications of being caught in possession of illicit substances. As we can see from the real-life cases above, these can be far more far-reaching than some youngsters may imagine, and it is well worth discussing with young people how getting caught with drugs could adversely affect the rest of their lives.

The Facts

Illegal drugs are categorised under the Misuse of Drugs Act (1971), as follows:

Class A Drugs

- Heroin, cocaine and crack, LSD, ecstasy, methadone (which has not been prescribed for you) magic mushrooms (if made into a preparation), amphetamines (if injected), cannabis oil.

- Penalties: up to seven years imprisonment and/or an unlimited fine for possession; life imprisonment and/or an unlimited fine for supplying or production.

Class B Drugs

- Amphetamines (if not injected), DF118 (tranquilliser), codeine and cannabis resin and leaves.

- *Penalties:* up to five years imprisonment and/or an unlimited fine for possession; up to 14 years imprisonment and/or an unlimited fine for supplying or production.

Class C Drugs

- Benzodiazapines, pain killers, sleeping tablets.

- *Penalties:* up to 2 years imprisonment and/or an unlimited fine for possession (applies to Temazepam in any form and Librium, Valium, Ativan and Temgesic if prepared for injection); up to five years imprisonment and/or an unlimited fine for supplying or production.

Drugs which are not illegal

- Prescription tranquillisers, steroids, poppers.

  It is illegal, however, to give or sell the above (with the exception of poppers), to someone else.

  Solvents are not illegal and it is estimated that every household contains at least 30 sniffable products. However, in England and Wales, it is illegal for shopkeepers to sell solvents to minors if they suspect the products will be used for sniffing, and in Scotland, sniffing solvents can mean young people under 16 can be referred to the Children's Panel.

Did you know it is an offence to..?

- be in possession of small amounts of a drug for your own use

- be in possession of small amounts of a drug which you intend to sell or give to someone else

- be in possession of large amounts of a drug which you intend to sell or give to someone else

- grow or manufacture drugs

- send drugs abroad or have them sent to you

- allow someone to use your home to use or sell illegal drugs?

Parents should be particularly aware of points 4 and 6, as they may find themselves being held responsible for their child's drug use in the home. What is important to note here is that:

- if you find what you think is an illegal drug, you must either hand it to the police or destroy it

- the police can search your house without your permission, if they have a warrant

- if a drug is found, the police must prove that you had prior knowledge of its existence

- the plant in your son/daughter's room which you suspect may be cannabis is illegal - and you could be prosecuted if it is discovered

- parents are not legally bound to tell the police if they know or suspect their children are taking or supplying illegal drugs.

The police can also stop and search anyone on the street if they have reasonable suspicion that the individual may be in possession of drugs.

School Drugs Policies

Many schools (depending on individual local authority guidelines) now have policies covering drug-related incidents. Of those who do, a great many will now automatically call in the police to deal with the situation. However, the school or the police will ensure the child's parents or guardians are also brought in and, depending on the severity of the incident (eg taking into account the type of drug and whether or not the child intended to sell it), this need not necessarily result in an arrest or exclusion from school.

But if a child is caught supplying drugs, this will always be regarded as a serious offence. Your child should know that even the good-natured youngster who volunteers to buy a quarter of cannabis to share with his friends and is unlucky enough to be caught, will be regarded by the law, the police, the school and the rest of society, as a drug dealer.

What happens if your child is held for questioning by the police?

- If the child is under 17 (or 16 in Scotland) the police should notify you where and why he/she is being held, and should not question him/her without you being present

- Your child is entitled to also have a solicitor present during questioning
- The youngster can be held for up to 24 hours (or 36 hours if the offence is serious) without any charges being made. After that time, they should either release him/her, charge him/her with an offence, or have a court warrant allowing him/her to be held for a further period without charge.

Cautions and warnings

If your child is not charged, he/she may be given a formal caution, which will not result in a criminal record. This means that a record of the offence will be kept centrally, and the caution may be cited in court should he/she be found guilty of another offence in the future.

In the case of a minor offence, a formal warning may be given instead of a caution. This means that a record of the offence will be kept locally for three years, and it may influence the decision to prosecute should another offence be committed in future. However, a formal warning can't be cited in court.

In Scotland, should any child aged 8-16 be held on drugs charges, a report will always be sent to the Reporter to the Children's Panel, who then decides whether the course of action should be a formal police warning or a Children's Panel Hearing. No criminal record results from either of these.

Prosecution

If your child is arrested at the age of 17 or over (or 16 or over in Scotland), he or she could be brought to trial in a criminal court. Being found guilty of a drugs offence means a criminal record for life - a sobering thought when you consider the following implications.

A criminal record for a drugs offence could:

- affect a young person's career prospects. Many employers are entitled to have access to a job candidate's criminal records (eg armed forces, emergency services, government agencies, employers with responsibilities involving children). Most employers will have plenty of choice when it comes to prospective employees - and most won't choose one with a criminal record

- prevent them from visiting certain countries. People with criminal records may not be granted visas for entering certain countries - a fact which could cause problems in certain jobs involving travelling, as well as curb holiday plans

- affect a person's ability to obtain life assurance or a mortgage.

Apart from the formal consequences, a criminal conviction can bring a lot of unwanted social baggage, too. For example, the youngster and his/her family may be ostracised by the neighbourhood, and this could lead to arguments, isolation and problems at school or work.

Summing up...

Potentially, a seemingly harmless experiment with a drug as commonly used as cannabis could have repercussions throughout a young person's life. For this reason, many people - including some police chiefs - believe drug possession offences (without intention to supply) should be dealt with in a different manner, perhaps through drug courts which would deal more leniently with minor offenders. This, they believe, gives problem users a chance to seek help, rather than landing them with a prison sentence and criminal record. But however you choose to look at the law's attitude to drug offenders, the present penalties can seriously affect a young person's future.

To be realistic, the long-term legal consequences of illicit drug use may be no more worrying to a fun-loving teenager than the long-term health consequences. Some young people will simply not care.

But we owe it to them to point out the facts about what could happen if they are caught using or supplying drugs. If they have this information, they can make their own choices. And, for some, the thought of a criminal record, or even of being in trouble with the police, will be enough of a deterrant.

Be aware, and make sure your child is aware, of the basic legal points outlined in this chapter.

- Let them know (in a non-threatening manner) what the penalties could be if they are caught using or supplying illegal drugs.

- Spell out the fact that supplying drugs is always dealt with seriously - and that the person who shares out cannabis or any other drugs with friends is regarded by the law as a dealer.

- Use the real-life case studies to illustrate how being caught with drugs has seriously affected the lives of some young people. If this has happened to anyone you both know personally, talk through the various implications it will have/ has had, eg on their career, travel plans, etc.

- Ask your child about his/her school's drugs policy - make sure they understand what could happen if they were found with drugs in school.

8 DRUGS IN THE FAMILY

- How can I tell if my child is taking drugs?
- If you do discover your child is taking drugs...
- Coping strategy
- Support is always at hand
- Summing up...

How can I tell if my child is taking drugs?

It's natural for parents to want to know how to spot the signs of drug use, so they can look out for the 'danger signals' in their children. But as we saw in Chapter Two, this is not necessarily a helpful approach, for two main reasons:

- signs associated with drug-taking can be mistaken for normal teenage behaviour, or other problems not related to drugs

- if your child realises what you're up to, it could betray his or her trust in you. Think about it from the young person's point of view: going through adolescence is a touchy enough business without feeling your every move is being monitored by an over-anxious parent!

That said, as a parent you are in the best position to notice if your child is upset or anxious about something, and if their behaviour is causing you concern, you have every right to try to find out what is bothering them.

Bearing all this in mind, here is a list of signs which may - or may not! - indicate that your child is having problems of some sort:

- sudden changes of mood
- uncharacteristic aggression or irritability
- prolonged loss of appetite
- lack of interest in hobbies, friends or schoolwork
- unexplained loss of money or possessions (including those of other people)
- lies and secretive behaviour
- prolonged bouts of tiredness or sleeplessness
- sores around the mouth and nose, enlargement of pupils
- unusual stains and smells on clothes

If you are concerned about your child's behaviour, you may find it useful to discuss this in confidence with your partner or another family member, or even a trusted teacher or family doctor. However you may feel about involving anyone else, it is always a good idea to talk to your child and show that you are concerned, rather than accusing them of anything. Try using the communication techniques outlined in Chapter Six to broach the subject.

Drug evidence

Although it's unlikely you will find actual drugs in the
house (and remember it is not condusive to a trusting
relationship to snoop round in your child's bedroom!), you
may come across the following evidence of drug taking:

- scorched tinfoil (not necessarily a sign of heroin or crack use
  - some people heat cannabis oil on tinfoil and then inhale the
  fumes)

- empty plastic bags smelling of glue

- burnished knives (heated knives are often used to cut cannabis
  resin)

If you do discover your child is taking drugs...

Throughout this guide, you've been advised not to panic
about drugs; to approach the issue calmly, and to find out
the facts. Understandably, that's not easy to do. Being
calm and non-judgmental about such an emotive subject
flies in the face of many people's instincts. It's hard for
parents to be objective about something they regard as a
dangerous threat to their children. And it's doubly hard if
they discover their children are actually experimenting with
that threat.

Parents who find out that their children are taking drugs
often experience a maelstrom of conflicting emotions: they
may feel angry, disgusted, frightened, disappointed,

bewildered, grief-stricken, hurt and depressed - all at the same time. The last thing they feel is calm, open-minded and ready to understand. But difficult as they may be to adopt, these attitudes are essential.

In the last chapter, we saw how staying open-minded about what a person is telling us can help us to understand them better. Understanding a person's feelings and actions can help us to help them understand themselves and why they are behaving in a certain way. They may also see how their behaviour is affecting the people they care for. There are no guarantees, but if they reach this stage, and know they have our support, they have a better chance of dealing with their problem behaviour.

We also saw that jumping to conclusions, preaching and laying down the law are natural reactions, but do nothing to help take the understanding process forward. Threats about calling the police or throwing them out of the house will destroy their trust in you and may make the situation far worse.

If your child is taking drugs and knows you have found out, he or she will need your understanding and support. You can give them that if you bear in mind everything we've learned so far.

Remember:

- you now know the facts about drugs. These will keep the hype and all its horrors at bay

- you also know there are various reasons why young people take drugs, and you can use this to help you understand why your own child is using them

- what's more, you've picked up some practical tips on

good communication, which will not only help you broach this difficult subject with better self-control, but will also help you and your child to keep talking

There is no magic formula which will 'sort everything out' if you and your child find yourselves in this particular situation. Every family has different ways of dealing with difficult issues, and, as we saw in Chapter Four, the reasons behind the drug-taking may vary enormously and perhaps require different responses, depending on how regularly it occurs and whether there are any underlying problems triggering it off.

However, these general guidelines may help you cope with the situation in a rational way, which can only be of benefit to your child, yourself and the rest of your family:

Coping Strategy

- Don't panic.
- Don't jump to conclusions that your child is a regular drug user.
- Don't fly off the handle. No matter how upset you are, try to stay calm in front of your child.
- Start talking. Tell them you know they have been using drugs and try to find out more. But remember, no Spanish Inquisition tactics - a sympathetic attitude will be far more helpful.
- Really listen to what they say to you. Look out for signs of hostility, fear, sheepishness or anxiety - these will give you an indication of whether the drug-taking was simply an

experiment, or done just for fun, or whether there may be underlying reasons such as unhappiness or pressure. Tell them what you think they are feeling in a non-judgmental way (see 'active listening' section in Chapter 6). Realising that you are not going to create a scene and that you want to listen to them may encourage them to open up to you.

- Use your knowledge about drugs to discuss some of the important issues. Let them know you understand the attraction, but ask them if they realise the potential implications - social, legal, healthwise, etc.

- Be realistic. Talking with your child will help reinforce your trust in each other, and will show them that they have your support. But it won't necessarily end the drug-taking.

- Seek the support you need. Trying to cope in this situation is emotionally very taxing. No matter how calmly you have behaved in front of your child, inside you will probably still be experiencing all the natural feelings of anger, worry, etc. You may also have dozens of questions about what has happened, but not necessarily wish to talk to anyone who knows you or your child. The good news is, there's no need to cope on your own. There are many people who can help you, no matter what your concern about drugs may be.

Support is always at hand

There are various kinds of support available to you and your child. The choice may vary, depending on where in the UK you live, and whether you live in a rural or urban community, but what is important is that support in some form or another is there if you need it. Here is a brief summary of the levels of support available. Contact details can be found in the Help List on pages 101-103.

Local professionals

Your own GP or local social work department will be able to advise you about the availability of services in your area.

National drug helplines

These provide confidential information and advice on all aspects of drugs and drug use, as well as information about legal matters and local services available to you.

Specialist drug services

These provide confidential information and advice on drugs and drugs-related issues (ie treatment centres, legal and housing issues) for drug users and their families, either by phone or face-to-face (some may use an appointment system; others may operate on a drop-in basis). They may also provide a counselling service.

Support services specifically for families of drug users

Among the services available to families are 24-hour helplines, one-to-one counselling, visits from drug workers, workshops and local support groups.

Hospital clinics

Hospital out-patient clinics throughout the UK provide

treatment for drug dependence (mainly heroin), which may include a methadone programme to help users come off heroin, and social work/psychological counselling support. The services provided differ from hospital to hospital, but most clinics are not generally in a position to provide help with other drug problems.

Residential services

These are generally for people with serious, long-term drug problems.

Summing up...

Coping with the knowledge that your child is taking drugs may be one of the most difficult challenges you may face as a parent. And, as with many other issues which confront families from time to time, it will require patience and a calm and sensitive approach.

If you can talk to your child about what is happening in an honest and non-judgmental manner, you have a better chance of facing up to any potential problems together, as trusting friends, rather than adversaries.

It may come to light that the truth about your child's drug-taking is not as earth-shattering as you had at first thought. Alternatively, you may unearth a deeper problem which requires professional support.

Whatever may happen, neither you, your child, nor

anyone else in the family, need ever feel alone. Never be afraid to ask for help. Whether it's basic information about drugs, someone to talk to in confidence, advice, or medical assistance, there are people out there who can give you the support you need.

- Be aware of the signs of possible drug use - but bear in mind they could also either be part of normal growing up, or indicate another problem.

- Resist the temptation to hunt for evidence of drug-taking in your child's room - it could spoil a trusting relationship.

- If you do discover your child is taking drugs, use the coping strategy outlined in this chapter.

- Never be afraid to ask for help - there are plenty of people who can give you the support you need.

9 COPING WITH A BAD TRIP OR OVERDOSE

- Golden rules
- Scenario 1: A bad trip
- Scenario 2: Heat exhaustion
- Scenario 3: Child is drowsy but conscious, and may have been taking drugs
- Scenario 4: Loss of consciousness or collapse
- Summing up...

It's every parent's nightmare. You find your child seriously ill, perhaps unconscious, and you suspect he or she might have been taking drugs. Would you know what to do?

An equally frightening scenario is seeing your child having a bad trip. They may be in a total state of panic, seeing terrifying hallucinations, screaming or crying, behaving aggressively, or even violently. Would you know how to cope?

This chapter will show you how to deal with a range of situations involving some form of bad reaction to drugs. Different types of drugs provoke different reactions and it's important to know what to do in each case.

The life-saving techniques described here are the same

basic skills used for a range of emergency situations, from drowning accidents to heart attacks, and these are skills which are in everyone's interests - adults and young people alike - to learn.

If you haven't already done so, it's well worth taking the short time it requires to learn practical mouth-to-mouth resuscitation and heart-start techniques. Short beginners' and refresher courses, and one-off workshops are available on a regular basis throughout the UK. See Help List, Pages 101-103, for details.

Golden Rules

There are two golden rules to remember in any emergency situation:

- Do not panic. It's natural, of course, but you must remain clear-headed in order to take control of the situation. Knowing what to do and practical experience of life-saving skills, will help you keep calm in a real emergency.

- If in any doubt, contact the emergency services. Don't worry that it may turn out that you've bothered them for nothing, or hesitate because of the legal implications of drug-taking. Your child's life may be at stake, and being over-cautious could help prevent a tragedy.

Scenario 1: A Bad Trip
- Symptoms: Panic, paranoia, anxiety and loss of control. These may be side-effects of several types of drug, and can be very distressing to both the drug user and anyone who

witnesses their behaviour.

- The drugs: hallucinogens such as LSD and magic mushrooms; stimulants such as amphetamine and ecstasy, and, occasionally, smoking a large amount of cannabis, are probably the most common causes of these symptoms, but they may also be caused by heroin, cocaine/crack, or taking a cocktail of drugs, perhaps with alcohol.

What to do:

- Don't panic, or get angry.

- Take them to a quiet room, away from noise and bright lights, which might increase their panic.

- Try to calm them down - reassure them that you are with them and that they are safe. Tell them where they are (they may be hallucinating and believe they are somewhere else). Talk slowly and soothingly.

- Panic may cause them to breathe too quickly (hyperventilate) or gasp for breath, which in turn causes dizziness, nausea and panic. Try to help them breathe normally by getting them to copy you.

- Stay with them until you are certain they have calmed down. If they are feeling sick or excessively drowsy, follow the steps given in Scenario 3.

Remember, if in doubt, call the emergency services, or, better still, if anyone else is present, ask them to do it, while you stay with your child. Give details (if you know) of any drugs taken, including alcohol.

Scenario 2: Heat Exhaustion

- Symptoms: all the usual signs of overheating, ie high temperature, flushed appearance, excessive thirst, faintness, collapse. Overheating and dehydration can become serious, life-threatening conditions.

- The Drugs: amphetamine and ecstasy cause excess energy and prolonged physical exertion, such as non-stop dancing. Those taking the drugs will not feel tired or thirsty, even if their bodies are, in fact, exhausted. Ecstasy will also raise body temperature, which is raised even higher by exertion in the hot, crowded atmosphere of places such as clubs and raves. Sweating can cause body fluids to be lost at the rate of up to a pint an hour.

What to do:

- Move them to a cool place - open all doors and windows.

- Sponge them down with cool water to help lower their temperature.

- Call for medical help.

- Give them water, but make sure they don't drink an excessive amount.

Scenario 3: Child is drowsy but conscious, and may have been taking drugs

- Symptoms: excessive drowsiness, slurred speech, possible confusion.

- The Drugs: depressant drugs, or 'downers', such as tranquillisers and heroin (not forgetting alcohol), and sometimes solvents, will slow the body down in this way.

What to do:

- Keep them awake and as alert as possible. Don't put them to bed or let them fall unconscious (the greatest danger here is choking on their own vomit). Techniques such as pinching their earlobe, keeping them walking around and asking them questions, will help.

- If they ask for a drink, give them only sips of lukewarm water - again, you want to prevent them from being sick, if at all possible.

- Call for medical help. If someone else is present, ask them to do this, while you ensure your child does not fall unconscious. If you are on your own, try to keep an eye on them while you are using the telephone.

- Stay with them until help arrives.

Scenario 4: Loss of consciousness or collapse

- Symptoms: can't be brought round.

- The Drugs: a variety of drugs may cause unconsciousness and collapse, particularly 'downers' such as heroin, tranquillisers and alcohol, or solvents such as glue or aerosols. A bad reaction to ecstasy or amphetamines, or overheating, can also cause this.

What to do:

This is an emergency situation, which requires immediate action:

- First, lay the child face upwards on the floor. Check ABC:

    A Airway - open by tilting head back and lifting chin.

    B Breathing - look, listen and feel for signs of breathing.

    C Circulation - feel with your fingers for a neck pulse.

If child is breathing and has a pulse:

- Move him/her into the recovery position (lying face down, head to one side).

- Call 999 for an ambulance. Give clear details of what has happened and what you think your child has taken.

- Stay with the child until help arrives. Cover with a coat or blanket, but make sure he/she does not get too warm.

If child is unconscious, has a pulse, but is not breathing:

- Do mouth-to-mouth resuscitation: clear any obstructions from the mouth. Tilt head back and lift chin. Close nostrils with your thumb and finger. Take a deep breath and place your mouth over child's open mouth. Blow into mouth until chest expands, making sure no air leaks out around the mouth. Repeat once (this will help get oxygen to the brain).

- Now call an ambulance.

- Continue mouth-to-mouth until help arrives.

If child is unconscious, is not breathing and has no pulse:

- Call 999 immediately.

- Do mouth-to-mouth twice.

- Check again for a pulse. If there is still no pulse, perform 15 chest compressions:

- Find notch at bottom of breastbone

  Measure 2 finger widths above it

  Place both hands on breastbone, one on top of the other, fingers linked

  Press down with full body weight (arms straight and elbows locked) steadily and smoothly 15 times, at a rate of about 80 times a minute.

- Repeat 2 mouth-to-mouth, pulse check, then 15 chest compressions, until you get a pulse and breathing.

- When they are breathing, put them in the recovery position and loosen any tight clothing which may restrict breathing.

- Keep them warm with coats or blankets, but make sure they do not get too warm. Stay with them, ensuring that they are still breathing, until help arrives.

Summing up...

The last thing we want to do in this guide is to make you panic. But knowing what to do in an emergency - and not just an emergency involving drug use - could mean the difference between life and death to a complete stranger...or to a member of your own family.

Now you've learned the basics, why not sign up for a short first aid course to gain some practical experience? Practising the techniques will keep them fresh in your mind and help you stay calm should a real emergency arise. And if the worst *should* happen and you find yourself confronted with a seriously sick child, keeping a clear head is the key to coping and winning through.

- Memorise the basic emergency resuscitation skills.

- Consider signing up for a short first aid course - and do it!

- Make sure you understand the different adverse reactions different drugs can cause and that you know how to respond in each case.

- Never be afraid to call the emergency services if you have reason to believe your child is having a bad reaction to drugs.

HELP LIST

Adfam National

(for families and friends of drug users)
Tel **0171 405 3923**

British Red Cross

(First aid training. A range of other first aid training agencies can also be found in the Phone Book or Yellow Pages).
British Red Cross Headquarters,
Tuition House,
5-6 Francis Grove,
London SW19.
Tel **0181 944 8909**

Cocaine Anonymous

Tel 0171 284 1123
Central Drugs Prevention

Unit (CPI)
Home Office, Room 354,
Horseferry House,
Dean Ryle Street,
London SW1P 2AW
Tel **0171 217 8631**

Drinkline

(London only)
Tel 0171 332 0202
Rest of UK Tel **0345 320202**

Drug Advice and Counselling Services (or Community Drug Teams)

(local details available from phone book, Citizens Advice Bureaux or libraries)

Drugs in Schools Helpline

(information service for parents, pupils and teachers)
Tel **0345 366666**

Families Anonymous

(self-help support group)
Tel **0171 498 4680**

Family and Friends of Drug Users

Tel **01926 887414**

Freephone Drug Problems

(dial-and-listen service giving details of drug agencies)
Dial **100** and ask for the above

Health Education Authority (HEA)

Mabeldon Place,
London WC1
Tel **0171 383 3833**

Health Search Scotland

(details of local support groups for variety of health problems and single copies of helpful leaflets)

Health Education Board for Scotland

The Priory,
Canaan Lane,
Edinburgh EH10 4SG
Tel **0345 708010**

Institute for the Study of Drug Dependence (ISDD)

(valuable source of drugs information)
32-36 Loman Street,
London SE1 0EE
Tel **0171 928 1211**

Lifeline for Parents

(free helpline for parents)
Tel **0800 716701**

Narcotics Anonymous

Self-help group network
Tel **0171 730 0009**

National Drugs Helpline

(free, 24-hour confidential counselling, advice & information - calls will not appear on itemised phone bills)
Tel **0800 776600**

Release

(specialises in legal issues
surrounding drugs)
Tel **0171 729 9904**
drugs advice line (office
hours) Tel **0171 603
8654** - emergency
telephone service (outside
office hours)

Re-Solv

(Information, advice and
counselling on use of
solvents)
Tel **01785 817885**

SCODA (Standing Conference on Drug Abuse)

(will give details of your local
specialist drug services)
Waterbridge House,
32-26 Loman Street,
London SE1 0EE
Tel **0171 928 9500**

Scottish Drugs Forum

(information on local drugs
agencies and family support
groups)
5 Oswald Street,
Glasgow G1 4QR
Glasgow

Tel **0141 221 1175**
Edinburgh
Tel 0131 220 2584
Dundee
Tel **01382 201016**

Turning Point

(drugs counselling service)
Tel **0171 702 2300**

The Welsh Drug and Alcohol Unit

4th Floor,
St David's House,
Wood Street,
Cardiff CF1 1EY
Tel **01222 667766**

Welsh Office Drugs Unit

Welsh Office,
Cathays Park,
Cardiff CF1 3NQ
Tel **01222 825111**

Parenting Teenagers
Make the Most of this Unique Relationship
Polly Bird ISBN 1 86144-018-9
£5.99 120pp Pub Sep 96

Parenting Teenagers is the answer to all parents'
prayers - a comprehensive guide to helping make
the 'teenage years' in any household as
pleasurable as possible.
Packed with information, advice and tips,
Parenting Teenagers is aimed at anyone who has
the task of bringing up teenagers - parents and
carers. It will also be of interest to those who work
with teenagers such as teachers, social workers,
youth leaders and so on.

Make a Success of Family Life
A Guide to Getting Along
Michael Herschell ISBN 1 86144-020-0
£4.99 120pp Pub Oct 96

A family can have many functions. At the root of
our family is our need as human beings to live
with other people; we need people for company
and for care. To be a successful family we must
remain flexible to the new possibilities happening
around us. This book can help you make the most
of your family by giving you ways of achieving a
fulfilling life together.

Get What You Pay For
A Guide To Consumer Rights
Gordon Wells ISBN 1 86144-023-5
£5.99 110pp Pub Dec 96

Simple, easy to read advice on consumer rights when buying anything from cars to clothes, from food to 'fix-it' services; whether face to face, by phone, or by mail order; whether by cash or on credit. Whatever and however, this book is a comprehensive guide to *Get What You Pay For*.

Stress-Busting
The Essential Guide To Staying In Control
Nick Daws ISBN 1 86144-027-8
£5.99 118pp Pub Jan 97

Stress has been described as the twentieth century disease. Contrary to the popular stereotype, the ulcer-ridden businessman popping pills as he makes multi-million pound decisions is only a small part of the picture. You can just as easily suffer from stress if you are a housewife...a factory worker...a civil servant...a driver...a police officer...a student.
Whatever your background, if stress is making your life a misery, help is at hand.

Need2Know

Thank you for buying one of our books. We hope you found it an enjoyable read and useful guide. Need2Know produce a wide range of informative guides for people in difficult situations. Available in all good bookshops, or alternatively direct from:

Need2Know
Remus House
Woodston
Peterborough
PE2 9JX
Order Hotline: 01733 890099
Fax: 01733 313524

Titles

____	**Help Yourself To A Job**	£4.99
____	**Buying A House**	£5.99
____	**Make The Most Of Being A Carer**	£5.99
____	**Stretch Your Money**	£4.99
____	**Make The Most Of Retirement**	£5.99
____	**Breaking Up**	£5.99
____	**Superwoman**	£4.99
____	**Work For Yourself And Win**	£5.99
____	**Forget The Fear Of Food**	£5.99
____	**The Expatriate Experience**	£6.99
____	**You And Your Tenancy**	£5.99
____	**Improving Your Lifestyle**	£5.99
____	**Safe As Houses**	£5.99
____	**The World's Your Oyster**	£5.99
____	**Everything You Need2Know About Sex**	£5.99